Littl...
Opposites

Read and Learn Sight Words

Zachary Moser

© Copyright 2019 by Zachary Moser. All rights reserved.

ISBN: 9781711161709

Little Book of Opposites: Read and Learn Sight Words
Read and Learn Sight Words Series - Book 1

Written by Zachary Moser
Illustrated and Designed by Jason Moser
Edited by Jason Moser
Published by Jason Moser

Hot

The fire is hot.

Cold

The ice is cold.

Big

The elephant is big.

Little

The mouse is little.

Tall

The giraffe is tall.

Short

The cat is short.

Day

The day is sunny.

Night

I see the moon at night.

Dry

The dirt is dry.

Wet

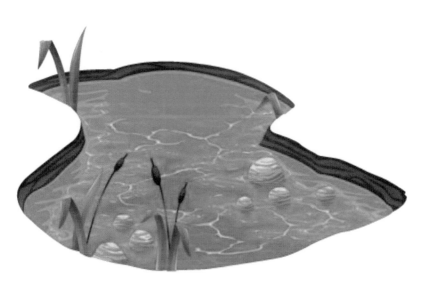

The pond is wet.

Full

The glass is full.

Empty

The bus is empty.

Near

I am near the
tree.

Far

The mountain is far away.

Open

The shark's mouth is open.

Shut

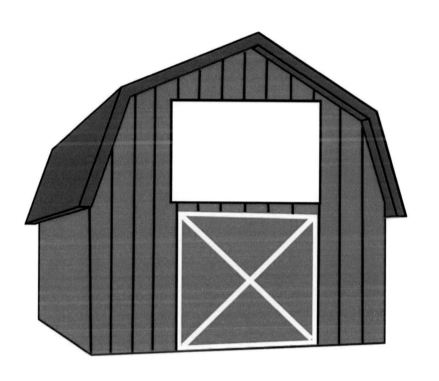

The barn door
is shut.

Deep

The cave is deep.

Shallow

The puddle is
shallow.

Inside

The cat is inside
the box.

Outside

The bird flies outside.

Happy

The snowman is happy.

Sad

The pig is sad.

Little Book of Opposites

Read and Learn Sight Words

Zachary Moser

Zachary is a bright young man just learning to read and write. He saw his daddy writing books and wanted to write books too. After bouncing some ideas back and forth, Zachary said a word and his daddy said the opposite. Daddy said a word and Zachary responded with the opposite. Once they had a few words on paper, Daddy found the pictures and Zachary wrote a sentence that corresponded to those pictures.

The trouble with most sight word books is the simplicity created with the pictures. A child isn't challenged to read when they can guess at the word based on the picture alone. In this brilliant opposites sight word book, the picture doesn't directly give away the sight word; the child must sound out the words in order to read the sentence.

Zachary is six years old and loves to read because of books like this. His brother Jacob, who is four, also enjoyed Zachary's book and for the first time actually showed interest with reading.

Little Book of Opposites

Sight Word Matching Game

Match the words on the left with the corresponding opposite words on the right.

Happy	Shut
Big	Outside
Day	Short
Deep	Sad
Open	Little
Dry	Far
Inside	Cold
Full	Night
Near	Wet
Hot	Shallow
Tall	Empty